Sir Cumference
and the Roundabout Battle

A Math Adventure

Cindy Neuschwander

Illustrated by Wayne Geehan

■■■ Charlesbridge

For Tom, Robyn, Danielle, Brek, and Hannah: a wonderful family
of ten when rounded up—C. N.

To Tomasz Modlinski Geehan and Olivia Modlinska Geehan—W. G.

Text copyright © 2015 by Cindy Neuschwander
Illustrations copyright © 2015 by Wayne Geehan

Published by Charlesbridge
85 Main Street
Watertown, MA 02472
(617) 926-0329
www.charlesbridge.com

Library of Congress Cataloging-in-Publication Data
Neuschwander, Cindy, author.
    Sir Cumference and the roundabout battle / Cindy Neuschwander;
illustrated by Wayne Geehan.
        pages cm
    ISBN 978-1-57091-765-3 (reinforced for library use)
    ISBN 978-1-57091-766-0 (softcover)
    ISBN 978-1-60734-766-8 (ebook)
    ISBN 978-1-60734-718-7 (ebook pdf)
1. Counting—Juvenile literature. 2. Rounding (Numerical analysis)—
Juvenile literature. I. Geehan, Wayne, illustrator. II. Title.
QA113.N48 2015
513.2'11—dc23   2014010499

Printed in China
(hc) 10 9 8 7 6 5 4 3 2 1
(sc) 10 9 8 7 6 5 4 3 2 1

Illustrations done in acrylic paint on canvas
Display type set in Caslon LT Std Antique by Linotype
Text type set in Dante MT by Monotype
Color separations by Colourscan Print Co Pte Ltd, Singapore
Printed by 1010 Printing International Limited in Huizhou,
    Guangdong, China
Production supervision by Brian G. Walker
Designed by Martha MacLeod Sikkema

"Another great harvest day! But wait—who's that?" asked Edmund Rounds, the castle steward. He pointed to a few small tents just visible among the trees.

"It's probably travelers bedding down for the night," answered Sir Cumference.

Just then the steward's son bounded up the stairway.

"Ah, Rounds 2, keeping track of everything in the castle?" asked Sir Cumference with a smile.

The boy nodded. Everyone called him Rounds 2, since he and his father were both named Edmund.

"Papa, I've finished the counts you asked for," he said, handing his father two scrolls. As the castle's next steward, Rounds 2 was his father's assistant.

"Wonderful!" exclaimed Steward Rounds. "Let's look these over during supper."

Steward Rounds studied his son's counts. "Hmm," he murmured. "Breads: 34 wheat loaves, 29 barley, and 25 rye. But the total is missing. Totals are important."

"I love counting, but adding up is always hard for me," Rounds 2 confessed.

"Let me help you," his father said kindly. "It's 34 plus 29 plus 25, which equals 88 loaves. And butter: 10 garlic pots, 20 salted pots, 30 herbed pots, plus 40 sweet pots?"

"100 pots!" Rounds 2 called out quickly. "It's easy when the numbers are groups of tens," he said.

"Yes," the steward agreed. "Adding by tens is quite friendly. But most counts are more complicated. As stewards, it's our job to know how much of *everything* we have in the castle so we won't run out. For example, there are travelers in our woods tonight who might need breakfast tomorrow. But let's get back to our numbers."

"Next," the steward said, "are the bees and their little homes, the skeps. There are 39 skeps, and—"

Rounds 2 interrupted, "The beekeeper said each skep housed about 1,000 bees, but he said not to touch the skeps—the bees can get angry."

"Ah, bees *are* difficult to count!" Steward Rounds nodded. "Sometimes knowing approximately how many is fine. But let's finish this up tomorrow," he added, noticing his son stifling a yawn. "Flit off to bed now. Honey-sweet dreams!"

As he nodded off, Rounds 2 decided that he would thank his father for his help by rising early to count the travelers. Then they would know how much food might be needed.

Just before dawn he slipped out of bed, tiptoed through the kitchens, and crept out a secret door in the castle wall.

As he entered the woods, he heard deep snoring—everyone was asleep.

He counted 40 men by an old log. Another 50 were near a campfire. A group of 60 was stretched out under a massive oak tree.

"That's 150 men!" thought Rounds 2. "Why so many?" Then he noticed a large banner with a distinctive insignia. He also noticed the tiny tents were full of bows and arrows. "Uh-oh," he thought. He sprinted back to the castle.

"Papa," he gasped, shaking his father's shoulder urgently. "The travelers in the woods—they have a banner of two hands clutching a chest of treasure! Isn't that . . . ?"

Steward Rounds sat straight up. Rubbing the sleep out of his eyes, he asked Rounds 2 to repeat himself. Then he leaped out of bed and grabbed his son's hand.

Steward Rounds raced through the castle, making his way to Sir Cumference and Lady Di's bedchamber.

"The travelers in the woods—they're Sir Wantsalot's crew!" Steward Rounds cried out.

Sir Cumference was up in a flash.

"Prepare to protect the castle!" he ordered. "Rounds 2! Fetch the bow and arrow counts while your father and I organize the archers!"

Rounds 2 raced to the steward's room and grabbed the counting scrolls. But then he stopped. The totals! Although Rounds 2 had made the weapons counts, he had not added them up.

Rounds 2 rushed to the artillator's room, seeking his father's help. But everyone had already left. He decided *he* must do the adding.

He thought back to the counts of the day before. "Why can't the numbers of bows and arrows be friendly tens like the butter, or approximate numbers like the bees, instead of hard-to-add numbers like the loaves?"

Butter Pots
Garlic   10
Salted   20
Herb   30
Sweet   40

Rounds 2 closed his eyes and tried to think. When he opened them, he saw a measuring tape curled in among the arrowheads, feathers, and string. It was lined with numbers beginning at 0 and ending at 100.

Rounds 2 grabbed the measuring tape and started using it to change yesterday's counts of the loaves of bread into their nearest friendly tens. Would the approximate numbers be close to the actual total? He took an arrowhead and placed it on 34, to mark the wheat bread. He could see that the arrowhead was nearest to the friendly number 30.

Bread Loaves

Wheat...34

Barley...29

Rye.....25

Total 88

Butter Pots

He then moved the arrowhead to 29, the number of barley loaves. It was also nearest to 30. Finally he located 25 for the rye bread. That was a problem. "It's smack in the middle between the friendly 20 and the friendly 30," he thought. "Well, the top line of the number five seems to point toward the next ten, so I'll make it bigger. Thirty it is."

Rounds 2 easily added 30 plus 30 plus 30. "That's 90, and it's very close to the 88 bread loaves that Papa added up yesterday at supper," he noted happily.

BOWS

	Actual Number	Friendly Ten
Long Bows	47	50
Crossbows	12	10
Short Bows	36	40
Total		(100)

ARROWS

Large Bodkins	77

Rounds 2 decided to add the archery counts in this fast, new, and nearly accurate way. He looked at his list.

"Long bows: 47. That's approximately 50," he thought. "Crossbows: one dozen. That's 12, so I'll make it the friendly 10. Short bows: 36, or about 40. So, 50 plus 10 plus 40 is 100 bows."

"Now for arrows," he murmured. "There are 77 large bodkins. That's about 80. The 23 medium ones would be approximately 20. And 98 small ones . . . Hmm, the closest friendly ten to 98 is 100. So, 80 plus 20 plus 100 is 200 arrows."

He was done very quickly. He looked at his list with satisfaction before sprinting to the main guard tower.

"They attack!" announced Sir Cumference grimly.

"Here," said Rounds 2 breathlessly, handing the list to his father, who passed it to Sir Cumference.

Sir Cumference and Steward Rounds studied the scroll.

"We don't have very many arrows," said the knight, a worried look on his face.

Sir Wantsalot and his men took aim.

Thwitt, thwitt, thwitt! Slender shafts streaked overhead.

A castle guard peered through an arrow slit. "They're busy as bees down there!" he yelled.

"Busy as *bees*?" thought Rounds 2. This gave him an idea.

He rushed to the rampart, shook the skeps, and pushed them over the edge of the wall.

"Bees, go buzz-erk!" he commanded.

As each of the 39 skeps crashed to the ground, 1,000 bees (more or less) angrily swarmed out and stung the invaders. Sir Wantsalot and his men sprinted away, never to return.

"That was a lot of bees!" exclaimed Sir Cumference.

"Close to 40,000," said Rounds 2 helpfully.

"Huzzah!" shouted everyone in the castle. "Huzzah for Rounds 2!"

"*Buzzah* is more like it!" cried Sir Cumference, with a very hearty laugh.

Rounds 2 continued to use his method of finding friendly tens when he was adding up the daily castle counts. He discovered that taking exact numbers and making them a little less exact gave him time to count and total more each day. As a result, he and his father ran the castle more efficiently. The steward named it the *Rounds 2 Method*.

Today we still use Rounds 2's idea. When we speak of a number and its closest round approximation, we say it *rounds to* that friendly number.